UNIVERSITY PRESS

Wild Weather

Ben Smith

Contents

A hurricane hitting Florida, USA

WOOSH!

Woosh! The weather is wild. This is a storm, a big storm. Big storms can blow over houses and trees. Big storms can be dangerous, but they can be very exciting, too.

Thunderstorms

Rumble!

Rumble! The weather is wild. This is a thunderstorm. Thunderstorms are common storms. Before a thunderstorm, you can see big, dark clouds. These clouds are called thunderclouds. A lot of rain and **hail** can fall from thunderclouds.

A thunderstorm forming

These are hailstones. They can be big or small.

You can see the lightning flash before you hear the thunder.

You can see **lightning** and hear **thunder** during a thunderstorm. In most thunderstorms you will see the lightning flashing first, then you will hear the thunder rumbling.

Lightning can flash between a cloud and another cloud, or between a cloud and the ground. A flash of lightning between a cloud and the ground can be up to 14 km long. A lightning flash between a cloud and another cloud can be even longer. Some lightning flashes can be up to 140 km long.

Thunder is caused when **lightning** makes the air heat up. Thunder can make different noises. It can rumble and it can crackle. It can **CRASH** and it can **BOOM!**

BOOM!

Hurricanes

s w i s h!

s w o o s h!

Swish! Swoosh! The weather is very wild. This storm is a **hurricane**. Hurricanes are very big, strong storms. They have very high winds and lots of rain.

Hurricanes are often given names.
This one was called Hurricane Mitch.

Did you know that the wind in a **hurricane** can blow faster than a car can speed down the motorway?

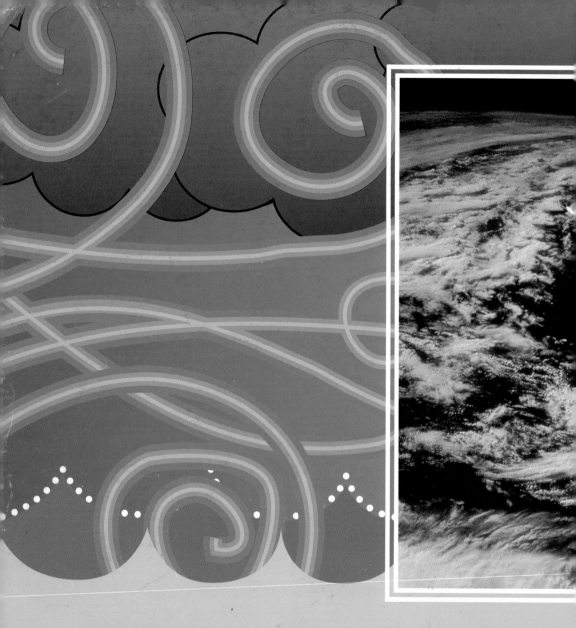

Hurricanes form over the sea. Warm, wet air rises up from the sea. This air forms clouds. Lots of heat comes from these clouds. This can cause thunderstorms, with heavy rain and strong winds.

These photos of hurricanes were taken from space.

This hurricane is over a farm.

Hurricanes are wide storms. They can be so wide that they stretch from one town to another town 800 km away.

The centre of a hurricane is called the eye.

The strong winds in a **hurricane** blow round and round. The centre of a hurricane is called the eye. The winds are not strong in the eye of a hurricane.

Hurricanes are wide and strong so they can cause a lot of damage. They can blow over houses and trees, and cause floods. There are two ways that hurricanes cause floods. Floods can happen because of all the rain that falls during a hurricane.

These houses were damaged by waves caused by a hurricane.

Floods can also happen when the wind is so strong that it makes big waves in the ocean. Sometimes, these waves are bigger than a giraffe. When the waves crash onto the land they cause floods.

Galveston

On September 8th, 1900, there was a very strong **hurricane** that started in the Gulf of Mexico. It blew across the town of Galveston, Texas. Lots of the buildings were blown down. The hurricane also caused big waves. More than 6000 people were washed away.

The waves crashed onto the land.

Tornadoes

Tornadoes are called twisters because of their shape.

Spin, Swirl, ROAR! The weather is wild. This storm is a tornado. Tornadoes are windstorms. They are very dangerous storms.

20

The tail of this tornado reaches right down to the ground.

Tornadoes form over the land. A tornado forms within a thunderstorm.

A tornado looks like a big, black thundercloud with a tail. The wind in a tornado is much faster than the wind in a hurricane.

21

Tornadoes make a roaring noise when they hit the ground. The noise can be as loud as the roar made by a jumbo jet.

Tornadoes are dangerous when they hit the ground. When a tornado hits the ground the swirling winds suck up everything in their path.

Glossary

hail – Frozen rain that falls in showers from heavy clouds.

hurricane – Storm with violent winds.

lightning – The bright light that flashes in the sky during a thunderstorm.

thunder – Loud crashing or rumbling sound heard after lightning.

tornado – Spinning winds that look like a funnel-shaped cloud.

Index